Lerner **SPORTS**

SPORTS
ALL-ST★RS

COCO GAUFF

Jon M. Fishman

T0018824

Lerner Publications ◆ Minneapolis

Lerner Publications Company
An imprint of Lerner Publishing Group, Inc.
241 First Avenue North
Minneapolis, MN 55401 USA

For reading levels and more information, look up this title at www.lernerbooks.com.

Main body text set in Albany Std. Typeface provided by Agfa.

Editor: Brianna Kaiser

Library of Congress Cataloging-in-Publication Data

Names: Fishman, Jon M., author.
Title: Coco Gauff / Jon M. Fishman.
Description: Minneapolis : Lerner Publications, [2021] | Series: Sports all-stars (Lerner sports) | Includes bibliographical references and index. | Audience: Ages 7–11 | Audience: Grades 4–6 | Summary: "Only sixteen years old, tennis prodigy Coco Gauff has played in the most prestigious tournaments in her sport. And she is only just getting started. Learn all about tennis's newest star in this high-action book"— Provided by publisher.
Identifiers: LCCN 2020026447 (print) | LCCN 2020026448 (ebook) | ISBN 9781728404370 (library binding) | ISBN 9781728418834 (pdf)
Subjects: LCSH: Gauff, Coco, 2004– | Women tennis players—United States—Biography—Juvenile literature. | Tennis players—United States—Biography—Juvenile literature.
Classification: LCC GV994.G38 F57 2021 (print) | LCC GV994.G38 (ebook) | DDC 796.342092/52—dc23

LC record available at https://lccn.loc.gov/2020026447
LC ebook record available at https://lccn.loc.gov/2020026448

Manufactured in the United States of America
1-48495-49009-10/1/2020

TABLE OF CONTENTS

WINNING AT WIMBLEDON

Coco Gauff serves the ball at the 2019 Wimbledon Championships.

Coco Gauff swung her tennis racket.
Thwack! She sent the ball zooming over the net at more than 110 miles (177 km) per hour.

Venus Williams stood on the other side of the court. The two players exchanged shots.

- **Date of Birth:** March 13, 2004

- **Position:** tennis player

- **League:** Women's Tennis Association (WTA)

- **Professional Highlights:** trains at Mouratoglou Tennis Academy in France; beat Venus Williams at Wimbledon in 2019 and at the Australian Open in 2020; won the Linz Open in 2019

- **Personal Highlights:** has two younger brothers, Cody and Cameron; played several sports as a young kid; loves music and funny YouTube videos

Coco returns a shot to Venus Williams.

Then Coco hit the ball deep, driving Williams back. Williams swung, but she couldn't hit the ball over the net. Coco had just won a set against one of her heroes.

Coco and Williams were playing at the 2019 Wimbledon tennis tournament. Coco was 15 years old, and Williams was 39. Williams has won 23 Grand Slam titles and four Olympic gold medals. She's one of the greatest tennis players ever, and Coco has always looked up to her. But at Wimbledon, Coco wanted to take Williams down.

Coco took a 5–4 lead in the second set. She served the ball 108 miles (174 km) per hour toward Williams.

After a few shots, Williams hit the ball into the net. Coco won the match! She dropped her racket and covered her face with her hands out of joy and awe.

The two players shook hands at the net. Coco thanked Williams for inspiring her. Williams told the younger player that she was proud of her and wished her luck.

Coco won two more matches at Wimbledon. Then she lost to Simona Halep, 6–3, 6–3. Coco's amazing success at such a young age proved that she was a rising tennis superstar.

Coco celebrates after beating Venus Williams.

Coco takes a shot at the 2017 US Open Junior Tennis Championships.

Cori "Coco" Gauff was born in Delray Beach, Florida, on March 13, 2004. She grew up in Atlanta, Georgia. Coco has two younger brothers, Cody and Cameron.

Coco Gauff with her parents in 2017

The Gauff family loved to be active and play sports. Coco's mother, Candi Gauff, was a star athlete in high school and college. She competed in the heptathlon at Florida State University. Corey Gauff, Coco's father, played four seasons of basketball at Georgia State University.

As a little girl, Coco took part in tennis, soccer, and gymnastics. Her father encouraged her to play basketball too. She tried it, but it was not the sport for her.

When Coco was about five years old, she watched a tennis match on TV with her father. On the screen, Serena Williams battled for a Grand Slam championship. She won, and Corey Gauff cheered her victory. He said, "[Coco] saw me jump up celebrating when Serena won, and she said, 'Daddy, do you like that? I want to do the same thing.'"

At the age of seven, Coco stopped playing other sports to focus on becoming a tennis superstar. The Gauff family made big changes to support her dreams. They moved to Florida, a state where many young tennis players live and train. Her father quit his job in health

Coco attended her first tennis camp when she was six years old. The camp helped her improve her tennis skills.

Coco watched Venus Williams (*above*) play at the 2012 US Open in New York.

care to become Coco's full-time coach. Her mother, a former schoolteacher, taught her daughter at home.

The next year, Coco played at a tennis tournament in New York. While she was there, her parents surprised her with a trip to the US Open. The family watched Venus Williams win an early-round match. Afterward, Williams signed a tennis ball and gave it to Coco.

In 2017, Coco became the youngest girl to make it to the US Open Junior Tennis Championships final.

Coco kept practicing and improving. In September 2017, when she was 13 years old, she played in the US Open Junior Tennis Championships. The tournament features amateur players from around the world.

Coco put on a show. She made it all the way to the final and became the youngest girl to ever make it so far. She faced 16-year-old Amanda Anisimova. Coco fought hard but lost, 6–0, 6–2. "I was hitting hard, but she would hit it right back," Coco said. Coco lost the match, but her performance proved that her future was bright.

DOING
THE WORK

Coco trains with her father before the 2019 US Open.

Coco's invitation to play at Wimbledon was the result of years of hard work.
She practices tennis skills for at least 12 hours each week. "I never have to say 'go to practice,'" Corey Gauff said. "It's always been her wanting to go practice and asking to go to practice. She's willing to do the work and never complains about the work."

Her father has coached Coco since she first picked up a racket. But he knew that to become one of the world's best players, Coco needed more instruction than he could offer. When Coco was six years old, she met with tennis coach Gerard Loglo. "She was so tiny," Loglo said. "She barely reached the net."

Coco was small, but she was impressive on the court. Loglo knew she would be a champion one day. Then he took the job as her coach.

Coco works on her serve during practice in 2019.

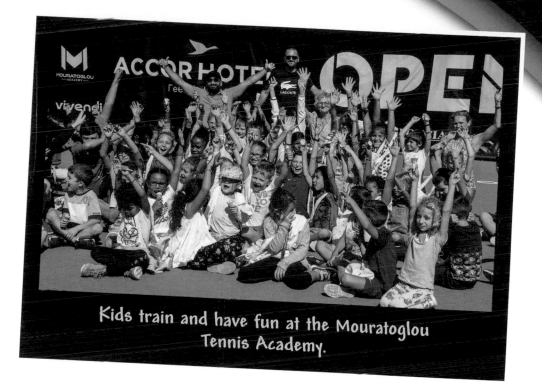

Kids train and have fun at the Mouratoglou Tennis Academy.

Besides practicing with Loglo and her father, Coco improves her game at Mouratoglou Tennis Academy in Biot, France. Since the age of 10, Coco has spent part of each year training at the academy. Patrick Mouratoglou, the academy's founder, has coached Serena Williams since 2012.

Mouratoglou Tennis Academy has many features for young athletes and their families to enjoy. It includes more than 30 tennis courts, a sports medicine center, and a luxury hotel for guests. It even has a swimming pool shaped like a tennis racket.

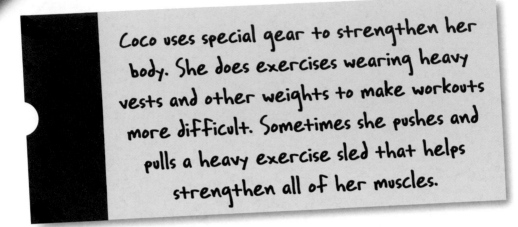

Coco uses special gear to strengthen her body. She does exercises wearing heavy vests and other weights to make workouts more difficult. Sometimes she pushes and pulls a heavy exercise sled that helps strengthen all of her muscles.

Yet despite the academy's comforts, Coco goes there to improve her tennis game. At Mouratoglou, she takes part in two group training sessions each day. A third session dedicated to fitness strengthens her muscles and improves her stamina. She also plays matches and has private lessons.

To get ready for the 2020 tennis season, Coco spent the end of 2019 at the Mouratoglou Preseason in Boca Raton, Florida. The event featured famous sports figures such as Serena Williams, retired boxer Mike Tyson, and fitness star Shaun T. The athletes played tennis, worked out, and had fun together.

Practices and workouts help Coco have power and endurance for her matches.

COCOMANIA

Coco cheers with the crowd after winning the second round of the US Open in 2019.

Coco maintains a balance of high-level tennis, training, and schoolwork. But she finds time to relax and have fun.

Besides homeschooling lessons with her mom, Coco takes online high school classes. Taking classes online allows her to study anytime, no matter where she is in the world. She might get her homework done early in the morning. Other times, she can't get to it until late at night. Coco says one drawback of online classes is connecting with her teachers. They're often asleep when she's ready to work.

Coco received an invitation to qualify for Wimbledon in the summer of 2019. To get into the tournament, she would have to beat three other players in qualifying matches. But before she could play, she had to pass a science test.

Coco loves music. She listens to stars such as Beyoncé, Rihanna, and Kendrick Lamar. Her favorite musician is Jaden Smith.

The crowd gives Coco a standing ovation
at Wimbledon in 2019.

Coco took her test late at night, just hours before the qualifying matches began. Then she won all three matches. She became the youngest player to ever qualify for Wimbledon. And she got a B on her test. A few days later, she became a worldwide tennis sensation by beating Venus Williams.

Coco's Wimbledon victory made her an instant star. She appeared in magazines and on TV shows. Suddenly, people recognized her almost everywhere she went.

Coco is active on social media. She has hundreds of thousands of followers on Twitter and Instagram. Before a match, she likes to watch YouTube videos that make her laugh.

After Coco beat Venus Williams at Wimbledon, people flooded Coco's Twitter account with messages. Pro sports teams wished her luck. She received notes from former first lady Michelle Obama, actor Reese Witherspoon, and basketball star Joel Embiid. She even received a shout-out from Jaden Smith.

Venus Williams (*left*) and Coco (*right*) shake hands at the end of their match at Wimbledon.

Reporters called the attention around her Cocomania.

Coco wasn't sure how to handle the excitement. After her Wimbledon success, people expected her to be great. The pressures of school, tennis, and the public's attention began to rise. She felt unhappy and stopped enjoying tennis.

Coco thought about her future on and off the tennis court. She spent time with friends and took part in high school activities. Before long, she felt better and focused on tennis again. "I came out of it stronger and knowing myself better than ever," she said.

Coco's parents watch her play in the second round at Wimbledon in 2019.

Coco prepares to blast the ball in the second round at Wimbledon.

"THE GREATEST"

Coco celebrates beating Timea Babos in the second round of the US Open on August 29, 2019.

Coco's first win in a WTA tournament came in October 2019. She finished first at the Linz Open and became the youngest player in 15 years to win a WTA event.

In the final, she beat 22-year-old Jelena Ostapenko in three sets. Coco said she would remember the moment all her life.

In January 2020, Coco played at the Australian Open for the first time. She faced Venus Williams in the first round. Just like at Wimbledon the year before, Coco won in two sets. Then she faced Naomi Osaka, the Australian Open defending champion. Coco advanced with another two-set win.

Coco's run at the Australian Open ended in a three-set loss to Sofia Kenin. Kenin went on to win the tournament.

Coco already serves with more power than many WTA players. At the 2020 Australian Open, she sent the ball rocketing at more than 118 miles (190 km) per hour.

Coco focuses on the ball in the first round of the Australian Open on January 20, 2020.

Coco hopes for many more future victories.

Coco hasn't yet made it all the way to a Grand Slam final. But she has many WTA seasons in her future. She's racing to the top of the tennis world. "I want to be the greatest," she said.

All-Star Stats

The **WTA** ranks all the pro women's tennis players in the world. Take a look at how **Coco** compared to other top-ranked teenagers in the summer of 2020.

Bianca Andreescu, aged 19, WTA rank: 6

Amanda Anisimova, aged 18, WTA rank: 28

Iga Swiatek, aged 19, WTA rank: 49

Coco Gauff, aged 16, WTA rank: 52

Anastasia Potapova, aged 19, WTA rank: 84

Varvara Gracheva, aged 19, WTA rank: 101

Xiyu Wang, aged 19, WTA rank: 107

Leylah Fernandez, aged 17, WTA rank: 118

Kaja Juvan, aged 19, WTA rank: 121

Catherine Mcnally, aged 18, WTA rank: 124

Glossary

amateur: one who plays a sport as a pastime rather than as a job

final: the championship match of a tournament

Grand Slam: the four most important pro tennis tournaments, which include the Australian Open, the French Open, Wimbledon (in England), and the US Open

heptathlon: a seven-event track-and-field contest

match: a tennis contest. A women's tennis match usually has three sets.

qualifying match: a contest to decide who will take part in a tournament

serve: throwing the ball into the air and hitting it over a net to start playing tennis

set: a group of six or more tennis games

stamina: the ability or strength to keep doing something for a long time

Women's Tennis Association (WTA): the governing body of women's pro tennis

Source Notes

10 Jared Schwartz, "The Serena Williams Moment That Inspired Coco Gauff to Play Tennis," *New York Post*, July 3, 2019, https://nypost.com/2019/07/03/the-serena-williams-moment -that-inspired-coco-gauff-to-play-tennis/.

12 Arthur Kapetanakis, "Anisimova Tops Gauff in All-U.S. Junior US Open Final," United States Tennis Association, September 10, 2017, https://www.usta.com/en/home/stay-current/national /anisimova-tops-gauff-in-all-american-us-open-girls--final.html.

13 Blayne Alexander, "Coco Gauff's Parents Tell Their Wimbledon Star Teen: 'Go Out and See How Good You Can Be,'" NBC News, July 8, 2019, https://www.nbcnews.com /news/sports/coco-gauff-s-parents-tell-their-wimbledon-star -teen-go-n1027266.

14 Jerry Bembry, "Coco Gauff, the Girl Who Would Be GOAT," ESPN, August 13, 2019, https://www.espn.com/espn/story /_/id/27381279/coco-gauff-girl-goat.

22 Abby Gardner, "Coco Gauff Opens Up about How Her Fast Rise to Tennis Fame Led to Depression," *Glamour*, April 17, 2020, https://www.glamour.com/story/coco-gauff-opens-up -about-how-her-fast-rise-to-tennis-fame-led-to-depression.

27 Chris Graham, "Cori 'Coco' Gauff: Wimbledon's 15-Year-Old Tennis Prodigy Who Has Been 'Raised for Greatness,'" *Telegraph* (London), July 8, 2019, https://www.telegraph .co.uk/tennis/0/cori-coco-gauff-15-year-old-tennis-player -wimbledon-2019/.

Learn More

Abdo, Kenny. *Coco Gauff*. Minneapolis: Abdo Zoom, 2020.

Coco Gauff—WTA Tennis
https://www.wtatennis.com/players/328560/cori-gauff

Fishman, Jon M. *Naomi Osaka*. Minneapolis: Lerner
Publications, 2021.

Smith, Elliott. *Serena Williams*. Minneapolis: Lerner
Publications, 2021.

Wimbledon
https://www.wimbledon.com

WTA Singles Rankings
https://www.wtatennis.com/rankings/singles

Index

Photo Acknowledgments

Image credits: AP Photo/Corinne Dubreuil/Abaca/Sipa USA, pp. 4-5; AP Photo/Tim Ireland, pp. 6, 7, 21; AP Photo/Chaz Niell/Icon Sportswire, p. 8; AP Photo/Corinne Dubreuil/Sipa USA, p. 9; AP Photo/Charles Krupa, p. 11; AP Photo/Chaz Niell/Icon Sportswire, p. 12; TPN/Getty Images, p. 13; AP Photo/Corinne Dubreuil/Abaca, p. 14; AP Photo/Lionel Urman/SIPA, p. 15; AP Photo/The Yomiuri Shimbun , pp. 17, 22, 23; AP Photo/Charles Krupa, p. 18; AP Photo/Press Association, p. 20; AP Photo/Charles Krupa, p. 24; AP Photo/Jason Heidrich/Icon Sportswire, p. 26; AP Photo/ Sydney Low/CSM via ZUMA Wire, p. 27.

Cover: Tim Clayton/Corbis/Getty Images.